EAS
IN
)(‿LS (

—

D0237155

WELCOME TO MY COUNTRY

Welcome to
ETHIOPIA

W

FRANKLIN WATTS

LONDON·SYDNEY

This edition first published in 2005 by
Franklin Watts
338 Euston Road
London NW1 3BH

Reprinted 2006

This edition is published for sale only in the United Kingdom & Eire.

© Marshall Cavendish International (Asia) Pte Ltd 2005
Originated and designed by Times Editions–Marshall Cavendish
an imprint of Marshall Cavendish International (Asia) Pte Ltd
A member of the Times Publishing Group
Times Centre, 1 New Industrial Road
Singapore 536196

Written by: Neil Macknish & Elizabeth Berg
Editor: Melvin Neo
Designer: Benson Tan
Picture researchers: Thomas Khoo and Joshua Ang

A CIP catalogue record for this book
is available from the British Library.

ISBN-10: 0 7496 6012 0
ISBN-13: 978 0 7496 6021 3

Printed in Malaysia

Franklin Watts is a division of Hachette Children's Books.

PICTURE CREDITS
Michele Burgess: 2, 5, 20, 22, 28,
    31 (bottom), 35
Camerapix: 3 (top), 3 (centre), 7, 10, 12,
    14, 15 (bottom), 21 (top), 31 (top), 32,
    33 (bottom), 37, 41
Ann Cook/MEP: 19, 43
The Hutchison Library: 8, 34, 40
Bjorn Klingwall: 1, 4, 16, 17, 18, 27, 29,
    33 (top), 36
North Wind Picture Archives: 11
Paul Rozario: 44
Liba Taylor: 24
Topham Picturepoint: cover, 3 (bottom),
    6, 9, 13 (both), 15 (top), 15 (centre),
    21 (bottom), 23, 25, 26, 30, 38, 39, 45

Digital Scanning by Superskill Graphics Pte Ltd

Contents

Words that appear in the glossary are printed in **boldface** type the first time they occur in the text.

Welcome to Ethiopia!

Ethiopia is the oldest independent country in Africa. A variety of **ethnic** groups, languages and religions are part of this country's **melting-pot** culture. Although once a leading African nation, present-day Ethiopia is rebuilding itself after years of **civil war** and **famine**. Let's visit Ethiopia!

Opposite: Addis Ababa is the capital of Ethiopia as well as the country's economic and political centre.

Below: These boys are from the city of Aksum, the ancient capital of Ethiopia.

The Flag of Ethiopia

The Ethiopian flag has three coloured bands. Green represents **fertility**. Yellow is for hope, justice and equality. Red represents bravery. A blue circle on the yellow band contains a star that stands for the unity of the people.

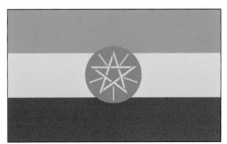

The Land

Ethiopia covers an area of 1,133,886 square kilometres. Eritrea and Djibouti lie along the country's northern border. Kenya is to the south, Somalia is to the east and Sudan is to the west. Because a large **plateau** stretches across the country, Ethiopia is often called the "Roof of Africa".

The Ethiopian plateau is split into western and eastern highlands. Mount Ras Dashen, Ethiopia's highest peak,

Below: Beneath the rolling hills of the Ethiopian highlands are some of the country's most fertile plains.

is in the Western Highlands. Mount Ras Dashen is 4,620 metres high. The Great Rift Valley lies between the Western and Eastern Highlands. Although the Denakil Plain at the northern end of this valley has very little plant life, the southern end is one of Ethiopia's most fertile areas. The lowlands west of the highlands are dry, and the Eastern Lowlands contain deserts.

Ethiopia has several major rivers including the Genale, Wabe Shebele, Blue Nile, Awash and Omo.

Above: The Denakil Plain in northern Ethiopia is one of the hottest and driest places on Earth. It has many salt lakes and it contains the Kobar Sink which, at 116 metres below sea level, is the lowest point in the country.

Climate

Different parts of Ethiopia have different climates. The lowlands have an average temperature of 28° Celsius (C). The highlands and the south-western part of the Great Rift Valley are cooler. Temperatures there average 16° C. The country has a long dry season followed by a short rainy season. About a month later, there is a long rainy season.

Above: The Omo River Valley receives a lot of rain. This area is one of Ethiopia's most fertile regions.

Plants and Animals

Lush forests cover the Ethiopian highlands. The lowlands and the Great Rift Valley contain tropical forests and **savannas**.

The lowlands are home to many animal species including wild pigs and dogs, antelopes and monkeys. Animal species unique to Ethiopia include the walia ibex, a type of mountain goat, and the Simien fox. Both species are **endangered**.

Left: The rich soil of the highlands is ideal for farming and cattle breeding. The cattle industry in Ethiopia is the largest in Africa.

History

Ethiopia is over 2,000 years old, but signs of human life there date back more than four million years. Ancient societies were farming in Ethiopia by 5,000 B.C. and were trading with Arabs across the Red Sea by 700 B.C. Between A.D. 200 and A.D. 500, Ethiopia became a major world power while it was part of the kingdom of Aksum. The Aksumites controlled almost the entire eastern part of the African continent until the Persians invaded in A.D. 572.

Left: The **obelisks** in the city of Aksum are over a thousand years old. The first obelisks were built in Egypt over four thousand years ago.

Left: According to Ethiopian legends, the Queen of Sheba travelled to Israel and eventually married Solomon, the king of Israel. Their son, Menelik I, became the first king of Ethiopia.

The Solomonid Dynasty

In the late thirteenth century, the Amhara people of central Ethiopia started the Solomonid **dynasty**. Its Christian rulers built a large empire, but ongoing conflicts with Muslims and Jews made the empire **unstable**.

Unity and Independence

By the 1700s Ethiopia had become many small kingdoms ruled by princes and generals. In 1876, however, a Solomonid emperor called Yohannes IV managed to reunite the country.

When the Italians invaded Ethiopia in 1896, the Ethiopian army led by Yohannes's successor, Menelik II, easily defeated them. The country flourished during Menelik's reign.

Opposite: Haile Selassie was the last ruler of the Solomonid dynasty.

Below: Emperor Menelik II led the Ethiopian army to victory at the Battle of Adwa in 1896. Ethiopia was the only African country able to defeat a European power and keep its independence.

A Country at War

In 1935 Italy conquered Ethiopia, forcing emperor Haile Selassie into **exile**. With help from Great Britain, the Ethiopian army **ousted** the Italian troops in 1941 and Selassie returned to power. However, his popularity declined after 1962 when civil war broke out in Ethiopia over a failed **alliance** with Eritrea. In spite of continued unrest and rebellion, Selassie held power until the mid-1970s.

Below: In 1935, Italian dictator Benito Mussolini successfully invaded Ethiopia.

13

"Red Terror" and a New Start

In 1974 a military committee called the Derg overthrew Haile Selassie and made Ethiopia a **socialist** state. Led by Ethiopia's new ruler, Mengistu Haile Mariam, the Derg arrested and killed many anti-government supporters in a campaign known as the "Red Terror". The Ethiopian People's Revolutionary Democratic Front (EPRDF) took power in 1991, bringing about the end of the violent Mengistu **regime**.

Above: The Tigray People's Liberation Front (TPLF) fought against Mengistu's government for the independence of the Tigrayan state in northern Ethiopia.

Menelik II (1844–1913)

As one of Ethiopia's greatest leaders, Menelik II united the nation with a strong central government and modernised the country.

Menelik II

Mengistu Haile Mariam (1937–)

After helping the Derg overthrow Haile Selassie, Mengistu Haile Mariam ruled Ethiopia from 1977 to 1991. While Mengistu was in power he had many of his rivals **assassinated**. When his power faded, he fled the country.

Mengistu Haile Mariam

Meles Zenawi (1955–)

Before becoming Ethiopia's prime minister in 1995, Meles Zenawi was a leader of the TPLF and chairman of the EPRDF. As prime minister, he has improved the country's economy and has made Ethiopia a democracy.

Meles Zenawi

Government and the Economy

After adopting a new constitution in 1994, Ethiopia became a **federation** of nine self-governing states known as the Federal Democratic Republic of Ethiopia (FDRE). Each state has its own president and assembly.

The central government has a Federal Parliamentary Assembly and a Council of Ministers. The Federal Parliamentary Assembly is made up

Below: City Hall in Addis Ababa is home to the capital's city council.

of two councils. The Council of the Federation has 117 members elected by the state assemblies. The Council of People's Representatives has 548 members elected by the people.

The prime minister appoints other members of the government. He is also in charge of the country's armed forces. An elected president serves as Ethiopia's head of state.

The Economy

A socialist government, civil war and poor land management all contributed to economic failure in Ethiopia in the 1970s. Even with the economic reforms made in the 1990s, Ethiopian farmers still cannot produce enough food to feed the entire population.

Nearly 90 per cent of Ethiopia's workforce is involved in agriculture. Farmers grow coffee, wheat, barley,

Above:
A farmer in the Omo River valley uses oxen to help prepare the land for planting crops.

cotton and sugarcane. Overusing the land, cutting down trees and farming with outdated methods have, however, ruined many of Ethiopia's most fertile areas.

Recently, mining resources such as gold, platinum and copper have been a growing part of Ethiopia's economy. Rivers are also an important natural resource for producing **hydroelectric** power in the country.

Below: One of Ethiopia's largest industries is the manufacture of leather products.

People and Lifestyle

The multicultural Ethiopian nation has many different ethnic groups that speak more than a hundred different languages. The main language groups are the Amhara, the Tigrayans and the Oromo.

The Amhara make up 24 per cent of Ethiopia's population. Amharic is the official language of Ethiopia's

Left: The Amhara live in Ethiopia's highlands north of Addis Ababa.

Left: The Oromo originally came from Kenya. They settled in Ethiopia in the 1500s.

government. Tigrayans represent about 8 per cent of the Ethiopian people. They live in the northern state of Tigray and work mainly as farmers. Approximately 40 per cent of the population are Oromo. These people form the country's largest language group.

Ethiopia also has several minority groups. Muslim minorities include the Somali and the Afar. Other minorities are the Sidamo, the Gurage, the Konso and the Nilotes.

Below: Tigrayans are descendants of the Aksumites. They speak two languages, Tigre and Tigrinya.

Country and City Life

Most Ethiopians live in rural areas. In the lowlands, they are often **nomads** who build temporary huts out of animal skins and river grass for shelter. In the highlands, they lead more settled lives as farmers, usually in simple houses that have dried mud walls and grass or tin roofs. In cities, most Ethiopians are small-business owners, merchants or factory workers.

Above: The Lion of Judah statue is a landmark in Addis Ababa.

Family Life

Ethiopian families are large. An average family has about seven children. In the countryside, men traditionally do the heavy jobs such as farming, while women cook and clean and raise the children. Children start helping their parents as early as age five. In cities however, these traditional roles are changing. Women often work outside the home, and more children go to school.

Below: Family ties seem to be stronger in Ethiopia's rural areas than in cities. This family lives in a rural community near Gonder.

Education

Education in Ethiopia is free but is not required. Just over 42 per cent of Ethiopian children go to primary school, and less than half of these students go on to secondary school.

Many children living in rural areas do not go to school. Instead, they are taught by their parents at home or by religious teachers at churches or mosques.

Below: This young student is learning English at a school in Harar. Many of the schools in Ethiopia teach the English language.

24

In most cities, children start going to school at age seven. Secondary school begins at age thirteen. Primary and secondary school each last six years.

Despite some improvements in Ethiopia's education system during the twentieth century, rural areas still do not have enough schools or teachers. At the same time, in some areas girls do not have as many opportunities to learn as boys do.

Above: Ethiopia has a low literacy rate. Only 43 per cent of the adult population is able to read and write. Some adults, however, go to night school.

Religion

Ethiopia has four main religions — Christianity, Islam, animism and Judaism. About 35 per cent of the people, including most Amhara and Tigrayans, belong to the Ethiopian Orthodox Church. Less than 8 per cent belong to other Christian groups such as Catholics and Protestants.

Left: An Ethiopian Orthodox priest is carrying an ornate metal cross during a Christian festival. Ethiopia is famous for these elaborate crosses.

More than 45 per cent of Ethiopians, including the Somali and the Afar, are Muslims. Muslim Arabs brought Islam to Ethiopia in the seventh century.

Above: With about 99 mosques, Harar is Ethiopia's holy Islamic city, but mosques are also found in many small farming communities.

Approximately 12 per cent of the people practise animism. Animism is the belief that objects in nature have spirits that affect everyday life.

Today, Ethiopia has only a few thousand Jews. They are known as the Falasha or Beta Israel.

Language

Although Ethiopia has more than a hundred language groups, its main languages are Amharic, Orominga and Tigrinya. Each state government can choose an official state language, but Amharic is the official language of the republic.

Below: The name of the shop on this sign is displayed in both Amharic and English, which until 1994 were the official languages of Ethiopia.

Most Ethiopians speak Amharic and either English or Italian, as well as their own ethnic group's language. Lessons in secondary schools are taught in English.

Amharic and Geez

For a long time, Ethiopian monarchs used Amharic, so it is also known as the "Language of Kings".

Geez is the classical language of Ethiopia. The country's most famous piece of literature, *Kibre Negest* (Glory of Kings), was written in Geez in the fourteenth century.

Left: This cross-shaped Bible is written in Geez. When Amharic became a more popular language than Geez in the fourteenth century, only scholars and the clergy continued using Geez.

Arts

Most Ethiopian art has a religious theme. Beautiful **murals** and stained-glass windows decorate Ethiopian churches, and brightly painted figures cover the walls inside. The influence of religion can also be seen in many other art forms such as the detailed wood or metal crosses that are used in Christian church services and processions and at festivals.

Opposite: The stone castles of Gonder attract many tourists. Gonder was the capital city of the Ethiopian empire between 1632 and 1855.

Below: Ethiopian art uses simple colours and usually features people with large eyes.

Ethiopian Architecture

The stone castles of Gonder and the obelisks of Aksum are some of Ethiopia's architectural treasures. The stone castles were built in the seventeenth and eighteenth centuries. Their designs were influenced by Portuguese, Aksumite and Arabic architectural styles. The obelisks were built during the **golden age** of the Aksumite Empire.

Below: The main square in Aksum contains more than a hundred obelisks.

Music and Dancing

Both music and dancing are important parts of religious and social life in Ethiopia. Some of the melodies that accompany Ethiopian Orthodox chants are more than 1,500 years old. Folk-singers, or *azmari*, perform at festivals and gatherings, especially in country villages. Special events, such as weddings and harvests, usually feature traditional dances.

Above: Ethiopians celebrate Maskal, a Christian holiday, with singing and dancing, often to drum rhythms.

Opposite: Ethiopia's skilled craftswomen weave straw to make baskets.

Handicrafts

Ethiopia's different ethnic groups create a variety of handicrafts such as jewellery, weaving, pottery and leatherwork. The Harari are expert silversmiths and basket weavers. The Konso of the Omo River valley are excellent potters, weavers and blacksmiths. The Falasha also make pottery, and the Afar of the Denakil Plain make beautiful leatherwork.

Above:
Body painting is a unique art form of the Surma and the Karo peoples. To make paint, they mix chalk and iron oxide in water.

Leisure

Ethiopians living in cities like to spend their leisure time shopping, eating at restaurants or going to the movies. In Addis Ababa they can visit the zoo or museums or the Mercato, one of the largest outdoor markets in Africa. A short distance from the country's capital are the lakes of Ethiopia's Great Rift Valley where city people can enjoy water sports, hiking or birdwatching.

Below: One of the places where Urban Ethiopians can watch movies is at the Ambassador Theatre in the capital city of Addis Ababa.

Ethiopians in rural areas spend their leisure time at home, either with their families or entertaining guests. Storytelling is an important tradition in rural communities. Not only is it entertaining, but it is also a way to pass on stories to the next generation.

Many Ethiopians like to play games that are similar to draughts, jacks and hide-and-seek.

Above: Mancala is a popular African game. The object of the game is to collect as many stones as possible in a mancala, a small slot on the game board.

Sports

Football is Ethiopia's most popular sport. Other favourite sports include basketball and tennis. Ethiopians also enjoy their traditional sports. One is *ganna* which is like hockey. Another is *guks*, a jousting game played on horseback.

Ethiopia has produced some of the world's fastest long-distance runners including Abebe Bikila and Haile Gebreselassie. Some Ethiopian female

Above: Football is played throughout Ethiopia in both country fields and city stadiums.

runners are known internationally too. At the Olympics in 1992, Ethiopian Derartu Tulu won the 10,000-metre race. She was the first African woman to win an Olympic gold medal.

Left: Miruts Yifter (*right*) won gold medals at the 1980 Moscow Olympics for the 5,000- and 10,000-metre races.

Holidays and Festivals

To Ethiopians, Christmas is also called "Ganna". It is celebrated on 7 January. On this day, Ethiopian Orthodox Christians go to church in the morning and enjoy a feast with family and friends in the afternoon. Timkat, on 19 January, is the most important Christian holiday in Ethiopia. It honours the day the Three Wise Men found the infant Jesus in Bethlehem.

Above: Orthodox Christian priests in Ethiopia take part in many of the holiday celebrations.

Ethiopian Muslims celebrate the end of Ramadan, which is a month of **fasting**, with a day-long festival called *Eid al-Fitr* or Feast of the Breaking of the Fast. Muslims also celebrate *Eid al-Adha*, or Feast of the Sacrifice, and *Mawlid*, which is a day that honours the birthday of the prophet Muhammad.

Important non-religious holidays in Ethiopia are National Day on 28 May and Enkutatash, the Ethiopian New Year, on 11 September.

Left: This Ethiopian is dressed like an ancient warrior to participate in a Maskal procession. Maskal is a festival held every year on 27 September. It celebrates the arrival of spring and the finding of the true Cross.

Food

A lot of the food in Ethiopia is spicy. Most dishes contain red pepper, garlic, ginger, coriander and other "hot" or sharp seasonings.

A pancake called *injera*, which tastes a little like sourdough bread, is part of almost every Ethiopian meal. Injera is both the bread and the plate of the meal. It is placed directly on a low table and a few spoonfuls of *wat*,

Below:
This woman is cooking injera on a stove heated with charcoal.

a spicy stew, are poured onto it. To eat the stew, Ethiopians tear off a small piece of injera and use it like a scoop. It is bad manners to touch either the stew or their mouths with their fingers while they are eating.

The most popular Ethiopian stew is *doro wat* which is made with chicken. Other stews contain beef, lamb or fish.

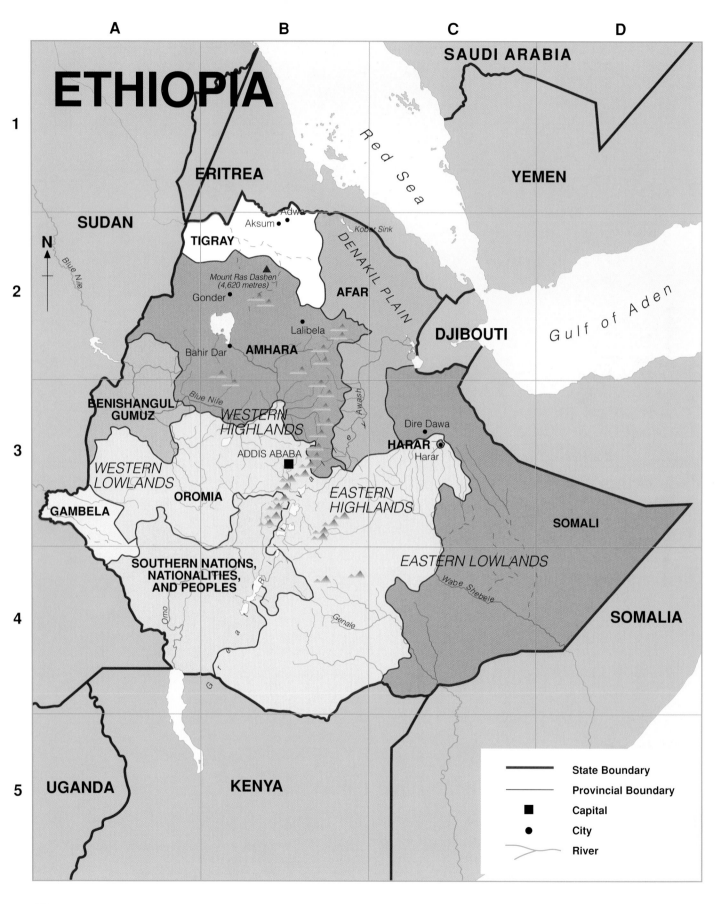

ETHIOPIA

SAUDI ARABIA

YEMEN

Red Sea

ERITREA

SUDAN

TIGRAY

Aksum •
• Adwa

Kobar Sink

DENAKIL PLAIN

AFAR

Mount Ras Dashen
(4,620 metres)

Gonder •

Lalibela •

Gulf of Aden

DJIBOUTI

Blue Nile

Bahir Dar •

AMHARA

BENISHANGUL
GUMUZ

Blue Nile

WESTERN
HIGHLANDS

Awash

Dire Dawa •

HARAR ◎
Harar

WESTERN
LOWLANDS

ADDIS ABABA ■

EASTERN
HIGHLANDS

GAMBELA

OROMIA

SOMALI

EASTERN LOWLANDS

SOUTHERN NATIONS,
NATIONALITIES,
AND PEOPLES

Omo

Genale

Wabe Shebele

SOMALIA

UGANDA

KENYA

	State Boundary
	Provincial Boundary
■	Capital
●	City
∿	River

Above: Houses in the town of Lalibela are built of stones.

Addis Ababa B3
Adwa B2
Afar B2–C3
Aksum B2
Amhara A2–B3
Awash River B3

Bahir Dar B2
Benishangul/Gumuz
    A2–A3
Blue Nile River
    A1–B3

Denakil Plain B2–C2
Dire Dawa C3
Djibouti C2

Eastern Highlands
    B3–C3
Eastern Lowlands
    C4–D4
Eritrea A1–C2

Gambela A3–A4
Genale River B4–C4
Gonder B2
Great Rift Valley
    B3–B4
Gulf of Aden C2–D2

Harar (city) C3
Harar (state) C3

Kenya A5–B5
Kobar Sink B2–C2

Lalibela B2

Mount Ras
    Dashen B2

Omo River A4
Oromia A3–C4

Red Sea B1–C2

Saudi Arabia C1–D1
Somali C2–D4
Somalia C3–D5
Southern Nations,
    Nationalities, and
    Peoples A3–B4
Sudan A1–A4

Tigray A2–B2

Uganda A5

Wabe Shebele River
    C4–D4
Western Highlands
    B2–B3
Western Lowlands
    A3–B4

Yemen C1–D2

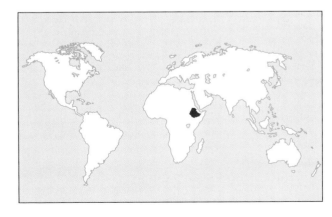

Quick Facts

Official Name   Federal Democratic Republic of Ethiopia

Capital   Addis Ababa

Official Language   Amharic

Population   67,851,281 (July 2004 estimate)

Land Area   1,133,886 square kilometres

States   Afar; Amhara; Benishangul/Gumuz; Gambela; Harar; Oromia; Somali; Southern Nations, Nationalities, and Peoples; Tigray

Highest Point   Mount Ras Dashen (4,620 metres)

Major Rivers   Awash, Blue Nile, Genale, Omo, Wabe Shebele

Major Cities   Addis Ababa, Bahir Dar, Dire Dawa, Gonder

Major Languages   Amharic, Arabic, English, Guraginga, Italian, Orominga, Saho, Sidama, Somali, Tigre, Tigrinya

Major Religions   Ethiopian Orthodox, Islam, animism, Judaism

Currency   Birr (16.11 Br = £1 in July 2004)

Opposite: This stone carving is a tomb marker located in the Eastern Lowlands.

Glossary

alliance: a formal agreement to cooperate for specific purposes.

assassinated: killed for political or religious reasons.

civil war: a war between sections of the same country or different groups of citizens within that country.

dynasty: a family of rulers who inherit their power.

endangered: in danger of dying out completely or becoming extinct.

ethnic: related to a certain race or culture of people.

exile: the state of being sent away by force from a person's native land.

famine: a very serious lack of food throughout a wide area, causing the people in that area to starve.

fasting: not eating at certain times or for certain periods of time, especially for religious reasons.

federation: a group of separate organisations or political states united under a central authority or government.

fertility: the ability of animals and plants to produce growth or to reproduce their own species.

golden age: the most successful period in the history of a nation or people.

hydroelectric: having electrical current generated by the power or force of moving water.

melting-pot: describing a place with many ethnic groups that blend or come together to form a single society.

murals: large pictures painted directly on walls or ceilings.

nomads: people who move from place to place within a region.

obelisks: tall pointed stone pillars with four sides.

ousted: removed or expelled from a place or position.

plateau: a large area of high flat land that rises sharply above the land around it.

regime: a system of government; the government currently in power.

savannas: dry grasslands.

socialist: related to a political system in which the government owns and controls the country's economy.

unstable: not firm; unsteady or weak.

More Books to Read

Africa. Continents series. L. Foster (Heinemann Library)

Africa, Europe and Asia. All about Continents series. Bruce McClish (Heinemann Library)

Conflicts: Conflict in Somalia and Ethiopia. M. Gilkes (Hodder Wayland)

Drought. Disasters in Nature series. Catherine Chambers (Heinemann Library)

Ethiopia: Breaking New Ground. Oxfam Country Profiles series. Ben Parker (Oxfam academic)

When the World Began: Stories Collected in Ethiopia. Oxford Myths and Legends series. Elizabeth Laird (Oxford University Press)

Web Sites

www.globalissues.org/Geopolitics/Africa/EthiopiaEritrea.asp

www.gondarlink.org.uk

www.oxfam.org.uk/coolplanet/kidsweb/world/muluken/index.htm

www.tourethio.com

Due to the dynamic nature of the Internet, some web sites stay current longer than others. To find additional web sites, use a reliable search engine with one or more of the following keywords to help you locate information about Ethiopia. Keywords: *Addis Ababa, Amhara, Great Rift Valley, Haile Selassie, injera, mancala.*

Note to parents and teachers
Every effort has been made by the Publishers to ensure that these web sites are suitable for children, that they are of the highest educational value, and that they contain no inappropriate or offensive material. However, because of the nature of the Internet, it is impossible to guarantee that the contents of these sites will not be altered. We strongly advise that Internet access is supervised by a responsible adult.

Index